A Collection of Thoughts

Alisa Niki

BookLeaf Publishing

Presentation by *BookLeaf Publishing*

Web: www.bookleafpub.com

E-mail: info@bookleafpub.com

ISBN: 9789357442671

First edition 2023

The Butterfly

It had a hard time flying
Torn wings but still beautiful
Another second chance had come
Slowly wrapped itself in a cocoon

Silky threads encased the delicate creature
Hibernation time had come
Waiting was the worst as there was nothing to do
Just sleep

Then time arrived
Slowly...
Peeking...
Peeling...
Unfolding...
The Butterfly renewed!

Spiraling

Spiraling through the darkness
Unable to see
Where to go next?
Unknown paths to take

Scared to move
Paralyzed
Tears flow often
Dreams shattered
Still spiraling round and round
Where I stop no one knows
So much potential lost?
Spiraling
Circles
A kaleidoscope of darkness
Spiraling

Nine Lives

I am like a cat
I feel like I have Nine Lives
I am on my Fourth Life
Four decades of living and Four lives

Life one was great
Full of energy
Young and spritely
Growing up and learning about the world
Lots of happy days
Close ties with my sister
All the way till end of high school until I got
sick

Life Two wasn't bad either
College was a time for searching self and soul
Stretching the mind past limits
Making memories and friends
Finding a boyfriend to keep for another couple
lives
It was a grand time graduating with two degrees

Life Three was medical school and marriage
It was rough but I found a loving time
Traveled the world

Saw so amazing things and experienced wonders
My husband was good to me
But as my body broke down I couldn't finish school
And that ended Life Three in a miserable way
I had PTSD after that

I am on Life Four now
Just starting over
Going through a divorce
Maybe that makes it Life Five or in between
Still… I'm finding myself over again
Lost completely right now
In the dark crawling and grasping
At least I'm alive I almost didn't make it
Now wondering what my other lives have in store for me
My Nine Lives

Meditation in Winter

Snow slowly falling
Over a Lake with Rocks
Rippling Water
White Blanket of Grass
Flurries of small cotton balls
A calm afternoon
No Geese in sight today
No nature sounds
Meditation in Winter

Sunrise

I wonder if you saw the sunrise today?
The orange and pink blush spread upon the sky's palette
The whispy clouds alighted from underneath
Puffy grey highlighted with Gold, and peach, and lavender
Clouds drifting, Bright light Blue peeking through once in awhile
I wonder if you saw the sunrise today?
It was breathtakingly amazing

Freedom

Freedom is a bird soaring through the sky,
peaceful and happy
Flapping it's wings with no restriction
Going anywhere, anywhere it pleases
Having no boundaries to where it can go

Freedom is a tree swaying gently in a breeze
Swishing to and fro . . . anywhere, everywhere
A rhythmic pattern coming from its branches,
telling the world "I am free"

Freedom is a flower, blooming
Unfolding it's petals, all it wishes
Growing and growing and becoming as mature
as it wants

Freedom is an exhilarating breeze washing over
you
A breeze that makes you want to fly or make
you happy that you're living
The vast space the wind can travel through is
freedom

Freedom is a river flowing over rocks
The water dancing acrossed the rocks, taking the easiest path it can
Rushing and running it shouts "I am free"

Freedom is the feeling of what you can do by yourself and what you want to do
Independence.

The Fairy Dance

A dozen fairies fall gracefully from the sky,
glittering and sparkling like diamonds,
Showing off by twinkling,
They swirl and do an elegant dance for winter,
They are made of intricate patterns engraved in
crystals.
As they twirl their tiny bodies to the ground,
they whisper a quiet chant ----------
Swish Swish Swish.
They make silent footsteps in the ground until
they settle.
Huddling together, they make a brilliant crystal
blanket.

To Be Loved

I just want to feel love
To be loved
Hugged
Safe
I am sad
Broken
Lost
Walking blindly in the dark
To be loved
Unconditionally
That's what I want
Need
Crave
Touched
To be loved
Will I find it?
Is it in me?
To be loved
Self-love
Self-care
Compassion
It comes from inside first right?
To be loved
I still want a partner
Someone to travel with

Experience the world with
Food with
To be loved

Dreams

The dreams I have turned into nightmares
Darkness
But I know there is light
Once there were sparkling high hopes to reach
Stars up above to catch
Now desimated and pulverized
Silver dust crushed in the palm of my hand
How time has been so cruel
Disabled by all the bad luck
Shrunken into a raisin
A try to rise again
Where is my Phoenix?
I must be strong
I know I have the strength and power
I am Woman!
Brilliant and intelligent still
Dreams will come again!

Me in Nature

Something needs to bloom again
My soul needs to open wide and heal
This flower that is my heart bled for too long
My inner thoughts have cried tears forever it seems
I felt damaged and wrecked like a boat that was out at sea

Change is coming
Not soon enough
Sunshine through the branches of the trees flicker
Hope of health and happiness
Strength
I am a rock
Solid
Balanced in nature
Trying to regain what I had lost

Fireworks

Fireworks bloom in the sky
Floral metallic circles of beautiful colors powder the dark night
Zipping and zooming
Flash bang
Leaving smoke behind
Starry speckles sparkling fizzles
What a spectacular display
Everyone oohs and ahhs
Waiting for the fantastic ending

Daydream

Clouds float by
Like a parade of puffy white animals
Embraced by the warm welcoming wind
On a sunny day
Meditative music whispering
Hair caught up wildly by nature
I am somewhere else
Flying towards an escape
Imagining the world is at peace

Ghosts

Ghosts haunt me
They tear at me and my soul
I am never free from the chains that tie me down
I wrestle with fears
Self-doubt grows from seeds into weeds
Am I still beautiful?
A hall of broken mirrors surround me
Spooky.

Save Me

Where are my angels to save me?
I seem so lost these days
I want to be scooped up by their heavenly wings
I need the sounds of their voices to guide me
Muses to inspire me to find a path in life
Salvage my soul from desolation
Find the light in my eyes again

Savor Life

Savor life like it's going to disappear
You only live once "they say" so live it well
Savor life and all the food
All the flavors one by one
Juicy fruits sweet and sour
Dripping. . .
Crunchy veggies crisp and bright
So many things to enjoy
Savor life and all the vacations
All the trips around the world
All the cultures
All the languages
All the art
The colors flying acrossed the room
The patterns created that are new to you
Inspiring views of nature
Savor life and all your friends and family
Relationships and lovers
They are our connections and our community
They make us who we are
Savor life because when our time is over we
want to say we lived well and we were loved
Savor life

The Cats

The cats scurry up and down the stairs
Their footsteps pitter-patter
They always make noises
But they are too cute to punish
They come to my bed
Come to curl up with me
Come to sleep and snore
Sometimes to my neck
Sometimes to my feet
They make biscuits sometimes at my neck
Sometimes at the soft blankets on the bed
They are so cute when they sleep
I have two cats
They get along well together
I also go to feed them for breakfast and dinner
They love their soft food then
Fancy feast is their preference
I want to make them famous some day
Maybe I can
They are good cats
They follow me around and love me well
I love them back

Night Stars

Can I fly to the moon?
Like a shooting star?
Twinkling and shining my inner light
Dreaming of catching a zooming comet?

Constellations painted acrossed the heavens
I always know where Orion's Belt is
I've seen an Aurora Borealis once too
Nature is marvelous
Night stars scattered and spattered amongst the dark sky
The mystery of the universe's existence
The puzzle of my own life

Goodnight

Now I lay down to rest my weary body
Cats there to join me
Calm in the darkness
Closing my eyes
Focusing on my floating body
Meditating on what's to come
Awaiting dreams to seep in
Trying to get comfortable and warm
Cocooning up in blankets
Turning on my heating pad
Hearing soothing purring in my ears
Heavy eyelids start to sink
Goodnight

Prayer

Knelt down to pray
Holding my hands together
Bowed head solemnly
Pictured an angel holding me for comfort
Gilded wings guiding
Soft light emanating and pulsating like a heartbeat washing lights of love on me
Gentle whispers of encouragement
A prayer to above that I will be ok for another day

The Wind

The wind swept acrossed the pond
Making ripples and waves
A hollow breezy sound blows
Strong and powerful it sways branches
A “Pied Piper” calls

Dandelion

Puff ball fluff ball in the summer
A light ball of seeds
People's wishes wrapped up in a sphere
A field of delight
Not a weed in sight
Even tea can be made
Jewelry hung from a neck dangles shiny hopes
Dandelion inspiration showers from above as
you blow away a bouquet

www.ingramcontent.com/pod-product-compliance
Lightning Source LLC
Chambersburg PA
CBHW051719130826
49812CB00034B/1256
* 9 7 8 9 3 5 7 4 4 2 6 7 1 *